THE CIRCLE OF LIFE PLAN

(The only journal you will ever need)

Alexandra Martin

The Circle of Life Plan
The only journal you will ever need

Copyright © 2021 Alexandra Martin

All rights reserved. This book or any portion thereof may not be reproduced or used in any manner whatsoever without the express written permission of the publisher except for the use of brief quotations in a book review.

ISBN:
978-1-80227-071-6 (Paperback)
978-1-80227-072-3 (eBook)

Introduction

You are here because maybe you are struggling in life or you have niggles in your life that you need to sort out so that you can behave in the way you know is best. Or perhaps you are just curious.

Whatever the reason, I am so glad you are here; you are so valuable.

This book is designed to be used by people of faith, whatever that faith may be, and many references are taken from the Bible. To those of us with faith, the power of the Creator is almighty and the Holy Spirit can guide our lives in the right direction if we allow.

The Circle of Life Plan is designed with this in mind and will be all that you need to get you through any struggles in life and how we end in this life matters most. I promise to use no jargon, no fancy words; just honest basic facts that will help you build resilience for when there are storms in this life and to help you ride those waves to come.

This is **your** personal journey and life as you are unique with your own fingerprint.

This Circle of Life Plan can be left for the next generation to learn from your mistakes and will be the most valuable earthly treasure that they will ever receive and leave.

Please complete this if you are able to, even if it's painful at times, as this will help you to the end of your unique incredible journey.

My Journey

Name: _____

Date: _____

PAST

Have you ever heard the saying "Like Father, Like Son?"

Your past doesn't have to be your future; it's how we end that matters and alongside every bad decision in life there is a good alternative.

How did we get here? Are we who we are through Nature (Upbringing) or Nurture (Environment)?

Always remember we came into this world with nothing and will leave with nothing although every one of us does have a special gift that can be used to make the world a better place. We are all unique and have different strengths and weaknesses and nobody is better than anyone else. We should also not blame others for our faults.

We all now have choices, and, although we may have chosen badly before, yet we can still make good choices moving forward. Throughout our life, no matter how unfair, these choices build the character in us. However, forgiveness is the key that allows us not to be bitter inside; after all, life is for living in peace.

Let's start your personal journey. Complete in pencil in case you need to rub things out and write things in different places. Mistakes are inevitable.

THE CIRCLE OF LIFE PLAN

Year of birth: _____

Date of birth: _____

Place of your birth: _____

Parent's names: _____

Brothers' and sisters' names: _____

Primary school you attended: _____

Secondary school you attended: _____

University or college attended: _____

Exams passed: _____

What can you remember about your childhood?

What is the story behind your birth? (i.e., what was your upbringing like?)

What do you think have been the worst experiences of your life?

What would you say are the best experiences of your life? (If having a bad day, think back to these good feelings)

I can tell you that even though you think you were not planned, you were, as you have a purpose in life defined by your unique set of skills.

You have your own DNA which could stretch from the Earth to the Sun and back, and our genes, which are looked at in a different section, make up only about 3 percent of our DNA.

To find out what your unique skills are, examine what pulls at your heartstrings and how you can convert that feeling into a purpose to help the next generation.

It doesn't matter whether or not you are well educated, it's what we do in this life to make a difference that is more important.

Never compare yourself with others as you don't need to; you are unique with different abilities.

Don't make a decision to follow others if the decision that comes from your heart is different.

Your treasure is where your heart is and if it is focused on money or popularity, then remember that these are only temporary possessions.

 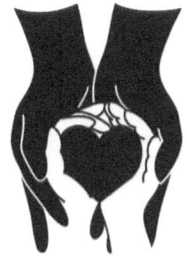

Choices

List the life choices that you have made which you think were bad and which you are no longer doing.
E.g., Got married too young, divorced, was a bully, went to prison, etc.

Now list life choices that you are still pursuing which you know are bad
E.g., addictions, abuse, cheating, lying, etc.

Look at your past choices – what would you have done differently?
If your past choices involved wrong career moves, you can still do what your heart desires.
Even if we know we have done horrible things, this doesn't have to be how we behave in the future.

PRESENT

Where do you live now?
_____
_____

Are you in a relationship?
_____
_____

Do you have your own children?
_____
_____

If you have your own children, do you think you are a good role model?
_____
_____

If a friend or family member were to describe what you are like, what would they say?
_____
_____

What are you not happy about?

_____
_____
_____
_____

What do you think you cannot change?

_____
_____
_____
_____

Look at your current choices that you know are not good; what do you think you could do to stop you from making these choices?

_____
_____
_____
_____

Are you carrying any burdens from your past? List what is troubling you.

_____
_____
_____
_____

Let your past be your school of experience.

Let the negative past die; you don't need it. Only refer to it when it is absolutely relevant to the present. Feel your presence in this precise moment.

Past experiences and early childhood situations can influence the way you think about yourself and others and how you make sense of this world in the present day.

You learn certain messages from your parents, other relatives, teachers and peers. Sometimes these messages are helpful and sometimes they are not. Sometimes, as we get older, we continue to live early beliefs and ideas and sometimes don't introduce core beliefs to replace the unhelpful messages.

If you get the inside right, the outside will fall into place.

Whenever something happens to you that is negative, there is a deep lesson concealed within it, although you may not be able to see it at the time.

When you are free from aggression and anger, enemies will be nowhere near, because you will be free and creating inner peace to experience joy. Revenge is not the answer and, if that is your intention, it will come back like a boomerang.

We will all be judged one day for how we end up on this earth so leave that aside and focus on the next generation by setting an example. Treat people how you would like to be treated. If you live as a perfect human being, then peace and joy will flourish in your life.

Earthly treasures are meaningless when you have not fulfilled your life here on earth.

If we do what we think is right then evilness has no room to spread. Think of yeast in bread as an example. Yeast, when put in a bread mixture, expands the dough; no yeast, no expansion.

Points to consider:

Real love doesn't make you suffer.

The light is too painful for someone who wants to remain in darkness.

Where there is anger, there is always pain underneath.

Now you have listed your troubles, what are you going to do about them?

Do you know where to go for support?

There is nothing too big that cannot be resolved, so do not fear as help is at hand.

If you have any problems with anything in your life that is not helping you function on a daily basis, or that is causing you stress and anxiety, the first point of contact is to speak to someone you trust. Find good people who can offer the practical help you need. It may be appropriate to use external local agencies, such as the Citizens' Advice Bureau or Samaritans, that can point you in the right direction, and any problem you have can be referred to specialist agencies. At the end of the day, we are not good at everything and even doctors, therapists and psychiatrists have struggles that they need help with too.

Don't believe everything you think because unhealthy feelings like depression can stem from unbalanced thoughts and beliefs. Cling on to what is good. Interrupt your negative thoughts by deliberately focusing on the external environment; then, focus back on the internal environment but his time, try not to hang on to the negatives. This will help you when facing threatening situations that can feed your thoughts, as this can result in bad actions.

If you believe, then call out to the Creator of this world who knows your unique DNA and is the only Master that you should ever look up to. He never changes and will always have your interests at heart. The rest will follow.

If your problems stem from your past, choices you made that you are not happy with or the things that you think you cannot change, then the Circle of Life Plan can help you. It will help you to be forearmed when the next problem arises.

Nobody can injure your soul and what is in your heart reflects on your behaviours as these are your thoughts and feelings. Believe that you were created and loved for a purpose and shout out to the Creator to come into your heart and help you.

The Circle of Life Plan will hopefully help you live in peace, joy and harmony; this will help us develop an appreciation of the need to respect the world we live in.

I will explain the Circle of Life Plan by assimilating it to the 'Lion King' film, which is about a boy's personal growth. The Lion King displays the ritual of birth, death and rebirth.

We all have a place in the Circle of Life Plan and this book will help you find a true place in that circle.

Dwelling on unfairness can feed unhealthy emotions and stop you from making things better for yourself. We are not saying that unfair things don't happen, because they most certainly do. However, life is unfair to everyone from time to time, not just to you.

Sometimes you face difficulties not because you're doing something wrong, but because you're doing something right.

Think about a tree and its purpose. Trees don't need humans to survive but humans would die without trees. Trees bring a sense of calm and can help us stand firm when troubles come.

Although trees lose their leaves and seem to be dead during winter, new buds and fresh leaves appear in the spring, symbolising new life and a fresh start. Even when trees grow old, they still create seeds that help move the earth from one generation to the next but in better shape than before. This can give us hope that we can put the past behind us and start afresh for the next generation.

Every time our bejewelled plant, the tree, completes another circle around the sun, the Creator of the universe gives the tree a new ring and 'tick' goes the clock - another year goes by. Therefore, when we see a small tree, we must protect it and save it for the next generation to climb.

Thanks should be on our lips every day! We can never say thank you enough to our family, friends, or anyone who has given us a helping hand. You will find that your attitude to life will change to become more positive, gracious, loving and humble. Thank the Creator for bringing you into this world and for the natural beauty around you.

If you feel the stressors of this world getting on top of you, take yourself outside your thoughts and focus on something that will take you away from the stressor. Go for a walk and look at what's around you or think of one of the happiest moments in your life to make you feel good about yourself. When negative thoughts enter your mind, try and focus on the happy times so the negative thoughts don't take over.

Deal with the difficult feelings by taking your mind to a calm place and focus on breathing in and out. Change is unsettling; sometimes it is necessary, but that does not make it welcome. Suffering is perfectly natural; it is how we deal with it that matters and how we act. Nothing happens to anyone that we are not formed by nature to bear. If you have pain, focus on the pain rather than avoiding it; to ride the pain is to manage it.

Life is not the way it's supposed to be. It's the way it is. The way you cope with it is what makes the difference. Look for even one small thing to appreciate - a simple meal or the branch of a tree.

Bad things do happen and often we can do little to change them. We can try to identify whether we had any responsibility for what happened or how we responded to the event. Perhaps take the negative situation and adapt and adjust to the conditions. Seek out positive experiences to deal with the negative ones.

Take time to reflect and think about the following statements and how you feel about them; write down your thoughts if you need to:

We all face choices – The choice will depend on you.
___
Are the choices you make harming anyone?
___
Anger should only be used for good action to express injustice.
___
Does your anger cause harm to others?
___
When faced with decisions, do you just think of yourself?
___
Making decisions should involve consideration of others too and the impact those decisions will have.
___
Outward actions should come from the heart, which holds our innermost feelings.
___
Children trust their parents and look to them for guidance and protection.
___
Mistakes and failures make us stronger and build our character.
___
Strong character develops as you struggle through tough conditions.
___
There are no triumphs without troubles.
___

Patience and having time to reflect can bring greater rewards.

We are responsible for the way we react to our problem.

Sometimes it is better to think of the long-term effect when we act.

Security does not come from wealth and possessions.

Have you thought of who can give you eternal life?

Whatever harm we cause on earth will be dealt with unless we seek forgiveness and heal ourselves from within.

If we don't forgive others then how can we be forgiven? Why carry the bitterness inside?

Never use others to benefit yourself because you will also be used at some stage.

Don't look at books and pictures or encourage fantasies that stimulate the wrong desires as today's thrill may lead to a lifetime of ruin.

Insecure people or uncertain people feel they need to prove themselves.

What matters is not so much the events or circumstances of life, but how we respond to them.

Further Statements

Humanity is better than status; focus on unconditional love.

Sometimes evil people are put in our path so that we learn for good purposes.

Evil sometimes attracts evil, but good news – evil will not last forever.

'Everything has a price' seems to be true in our world of bribes, desire for wealth and materialism.

The Creator is in control far beyond our immediate circumstances.

Don't be a slave to wrong-doing; enjoy peace, joy and harmony with others.

Our background does not have to be our future.

Our unique qualities can make a difference to this world.

Don't be motivated by greed; instead, use your possessions to help others.

We are sometimes not responsible for what happens to us but our response is important.

Great opportunities are often destroyed by small decisions.

Sometimes you go your own way instead of evaluating the advice given.

Sometimes going your own way leaves you open to exploitation.

Thoughtless decisions often lead to exchanging something more valuable for something less valuable.

Selfishness, left unchecked, can lead to great evil.

Sometimes we avoid doing what is right because of what others might think.

As we recognise what is pulling at our heart-strings, the deep needs of our world, we can help by putting together a plan of action.

We should adjust our minds and attitudes by treating people the way we would like to be treated.

The person on the receiving end will be affected by our actions.

Although we fight battles every day, we can be assured that the battle is won as we can have eternal life if we believe in our Creator.

Ask for forgiveness for what we have done wrong and start afresh.

Further statements

Be careful to put your trust in people who are trustworthy, not those who are using you for personal gain.

Chose people with qualities you would like to develop in your own life.

Do the right thing at the right time and always think of others so that your action will have the right impact.

Do you go along with the crowd or speak up if something is wrong?

Those who view children as a distraction or nuisance should instead look on them as an opportunity to shape the future.

We may inherit our parent's or relative's money but we cannot inherit a good character.

We must know what the right actions are by accepting the right advice.

The kind of person we are is more important than what we do.
Look to your heart; what comes from the mouth, comes from our heart.

Our weaknesses remind us that we need help, so admit what they are and deal with them.

Life's tough situations can bring out the best in people as they take our focus away from earthly rewards.

Trouble can be a blessing to make us stronger; this may be presented in unlikely circumstances.

We sometimes have to do a 180-degree turn from the kind of self-centeredness that leads to lying, cheating, stealing, gossiping, taking revenge, abusing and indulging in sexual immorality.

People tend to follow false Gods of technology, materialism and war; instead, focus on the creation, not the creator.

Those who seek status and importance here will have nothing in eternity; however, the people who have served others will.

If your heart is committed to peace, joy and love, you will accomplish what you have set out to do as it will change people's lives for the better.

As helpful or hurtful as others may be, we are individually responsible for what we do.

Further statements

We should no longer prove ourselves to others; trust your own instincts to know what is good.

We must not let comfort, security or material possessions overshadow right from wrong.

Run from everything that is wrong and chose to do what is right. Running from a tempting situation is the first step to victory.

Sometimes people are so obsessed with money that it controls their life.

Sometimes, when our plans don't work out as we want them to, they work out even better than we expected.

Things rot, rust and decay; why focus on earthly treasures?

What we feed our mind influences our total health and well-being.

When you go with the decision that pulls at your heartstrings, and your actions are put to good use, you don't need to compare yourself to others.

When making decisions, get the facts before answering; make sure you hear both sides, then it should end only in good.

Do not surrender to the stress but remain resilient and recover from setbacks.

Children who have everything also lack purpose and direction in their lives.

Our heritage can sometimes determine our life decisions, as in the life of the Prince of Wales, for example. However, heritage does not always determine them, as in the decisions made by Prince Harry.

Many people use religion to gain prestige, comfort or even political votes, but those are self-centred motives. True believers know the truth and the way they should live.

The real value of a person is inside, not outside.

Use your anger to find constructive solutions rather than to tear people down.

You can tell a lot about a person from the way they handle money. The evil people only focus on it, while the righteous use it to help others in need. There is no excuse.

We may not walk on water but we do walk through storms.

Sometimes, the twisted motives and actions of our enemies will be used to better us.

Sometimes, easy choices allow us to be lazy.

As our bodies hunger and thirst, so do our souls.
___

Admitting to our mistakes gives us the strength to move forward.
___

Words to think about.

If you ask the Holy Spirit for what you really want, don't be surprised when you are given what you really need.

The Holy Spirit's work in our lives is to achieve deep and lasting peace so that we never need to fear the present or the future.

If Jesus had not died for our sins and gone back to the Father, our Creator, then the Holy Spirit would not have been with us today to have a personal relationship. Our Creator's (God) first breath made man different from all other forms of creation. Now, through the breath of Jesus, God imparted eternal, spiritual life. With this inbreathing came the power to do God's will on earth through the Holy Spirit.

When evidence is presented to us in a courtroom, those who hear it must make a choice. You are now the jury; you either believe the evidence of the bible (John's Gospel) or you don't. Only you can decide.

If Jesus had stayed on earth, his physical presence would have limited the spread of the gospel because he could only be in one place at a time. After Christ was taken up into heaven, he would be spiritually present everywhere through the Holy Spirit. The spirit would be comforting and give the right words to say and fill with power.

The world hates believers because their values are different and they don't join in the world's sin; that is Satan's agenda.

Watch out for what you say, always speak the truth and control your tongue.

What you do under pressure often shows what you are really like.

Our actions and our attitudes must be sincere; it is what we think and say that makes us unclean.

Concentrate on what is right and feels good and you, more often than not, will choose the right people to be around you.

You will attract good friends because your attitude is right.

Look for opportunities that can fulfil your strengths, as this will allow you to contribute wholeheartedly to this world to make it a better place for the next generation.

Sometimes, we do not fulfil what is pulling at our heartstrings as the vision has ended before it became a reality, but we can help someone else to carry out their vision by preparing and encouraging others.

We have unique qualities that can make a difference to this world and can be passed to the next generation

For good or evil, families have a lasting and powerful influence on their children. Traits and qualities are passed on to the next generation and often the mistakes and sins of the parents are repeated by the children.

Our failures help us get back up and it's never too late to start again.

Words of encouragement.

Life's tough situations can bring out the best in people.

Little decisions could be part of a big plan.

Sickness and Evil are consequences of living in a fallen world

Why are some children physically disabled and other children athletically gifted? Why do people die before reaching their potential? Questions like this cannot be answered because we cannot see all that God sees. He has chosen to allow evil in this world for a time, but we can trust that God will destroy all evil eventually. In the meantime, God will help us to use our suffering to strengthen us.

Angels are God's messengers with supernatural powers and they sometimes take on human appearance in order to talk to people.

We live in a fallen world where good behaviour is not always rewarded and bad behaviour not always punished. Therefore, innocent people sometimes suffer, but if any suffering was taken away from us when we asked, we would not ever experience love and devotion but would be strengthened for the next time.

The kind of person we are is more important than anything we might do.

We must not turn our backs on people who are repulsive to us or who don't live up to our standards, as we must realise that every human individual is a unique creation.

Talk is cheap; we must walk the talk. Our words are meaningless if our actions don't back us up.

Think of a person that you liked who was kind, who has now departed and who has had an influence on you.

We suffer for many reasons – our own mistakes, someone else's mistakes, injustice. When we suffer from our own mistakes, we get what we deserve if we have repeated them. When we suffer because of others or because of injustice, don't seek revenge as this is not your battle.

Weaknesses should help us remember that we need support from others as our strengths are unique and we should make use of both; remember, we were created with different gifts.

We may think we go unnoticed and devalued by others but we are special and loved by our Creator, who just wants a personal relationship with you and wants your heart.

Opportunities and successes in this life are temporary; remember to find a balance in your life to do some good.

Careless efforts to correct errors often lead to the same errors.

Mistakes occur when we attempt to take over the situation without thinking it through.

Words that you might take advice from.

To learn from an error, we need to admit it and make adjustments so that it doesn't happen again; everyone makes mistakes but fools repeat them.

If we follow corrupt leaders knowingly, we can't excuse ourselves by blaming their bad example, but do not fret as there is nothing that is hidden that will not be disclosed.

Unfairly getting a promotion, passing an exam, or gaining something will never bring lasting happiness.

Having too much money can be dangerous, but so can having too little. Being poor can, in fact, be hazardous to physical as well as spiritual health. Neither poverty nor riches is effective but finding a balance is the key.

If you work solely for money and to gain possessions, not only will everything be left behind at death, but it may be left to those who have done nothing to deserve it and will spoil it, which will not guide them through life's complications. People who abuse their possessions will end up with nothing.

Food costs money, lasts only a short time, and meets only physical needs. What are you using to nourish your soul that doesn't include personal greed?

If we use our money to help those in need, our earthly investment will bring eternal benefit; heavenly riches are far more valuable than earthly wealth.

Before you send money to any cause, evaluate it carefully. Is the money being used to promote someone's own interests and luxurious lifestyle?

False security is those clinging to this life seeking to escape physical persecution. They live for themselves and display common attitudes, which include materialism – I want it and work hard to get it, so it's mine. All that I see is real and unseen things are just dreams.

Don't dwell on the things that you have given up; think about what you have gained.

Where our commitment lies makes a great difference because it can result in recklessness.

One measure of greatness is the willingness to serve the poor as well as the most powerful.

We should use our humble heart to make a difference and a purpose.

Think of the world as a field; seeds are sown; the weeds are the evil ones and the wheat are the good ones that produce a good crop and the harvesters are the angels; the seed on the good soil stands for those with a noble and good heart. Remember, not every seed lands on good soil.

A good and hopeful start can be ruined by an evil end if we do not make wise decisions.

Words that might help you make better choices.

Before jumping into a project, check the ideas will work and are realistic then you will be able to plan with confidence.

The opportunities we have are more important than the ones we wish we had.

When you encourage and motivate others, you put teamwork into action and accomplish goals, as each person has a meaning and purpose to get the job done.

Don't cut yourself off from others. Instead, join others as they need you as much as you need them; we have different gifts.

Some people or things that seem like obvious sources of help or relief may turn out to be controlling instead. Trust is the key; follow your heart; you will know when someone is not right for you.

We need people around us who will not just discuss a situation but will do something about it.

The way we help those in need says a lot about us as a person.

A muscle grows stronger if exercised but an unused muscle grows weak. How are you using your strength, to help or to do nothing?

We are not intended to profit from people's misfortune; caring for someone is more important than personal gain.

We should generally help people, not exploit them.

People today are just eager to raise their social status, whether by being with the right people, dressing for success, or driving the right car. Who are you trying to impress? Serving people is more important than success

A friend who has your best interests at heart may have to give you unpleasant advice at times but you know it is for your own good.

A person who feels worthy will always do more than expected.

When allowed to run its course, evil destroys itself.

Many in our world today mock the supernatural. They deny the reality of the spiritual world and claim that only what can be seen and felt is real, but they will be proven wrong in the end.

A person is a slave to whatever controls them.

Lying about someone is an act of physical violence. Its effects can be as permanent as a stab wound, so next time you are thinking of lying, imagine stabbing this person.

Think of the first prick of a thorn; we remove it before it damages us. Don't let the thorn get to the flesh.

Words that may highlight something in your life.

If someone annoys you, decide not to complain about the person and see if the irritation dies from lack of fuel.

People sometimes hate you if you show them what is wrong because they know you are a threat to their selfish gain.

The truth sometimes stings, but our reaction to the truth shows what we are made of; we can take the truth humbly to heart and let it change us.

When you ask for help, consider your motive; is it for justice or is it to make you feel good about yourself\?

When the task ahead seems like a mountain to climb, take small steps and strength will be given to climb to the top.

Our troubles can be helpful as they can humble us.

In certain situations that we find ourselves in that do not go to plan, there may be a better solution on its way.

One of the best moments in life is when you find the courage to let go of what you cannot change.

There is no need to rush things; what is meant for you will arrive on time.

Don't doubt things; remember how far you have come.

Only you decide what you can do with your time; you can move forward or focus on using up negative energy.

Walk away from arguments that lead you to anger unless the anger is to fight injustice.

The more you walk away from things that poison your soul, the healthier you will be.

The beginning of the spiritual process is to admit you need help to be renewed and seek forgiveness for your wrongdoing.

Ideas of eternal life are based on images of human thoughts. Concentrate on the Creator and about what heaven will look like instead.

Difficult roads often lead to beautiful destinations.

Nothing is hidden in this world; do not seek revenge as justice will be dealt with.

Lessons in life that can help you with your behaviours and choosing right from wrong, and not being pressured into making wrong decisions

If you are struggling with a decision, seek an older wise person whom you can trust, and if you believe, the Creator will always put someone in your path.

The choice of a partner in life will have a significant effect on life, physically, spiritually and emotionally.

Anyone can accomplish many things by using the gifts and special abilities that they have been given.

When you face difficult situations and feel surrounded, outnumbered, overpowered or outclassed, remember, just do what you feel is right. This will come from your heart and your conscience will be clear as what comes out from within matters.

Keep up appearances while your private world is corrupt, but what is said in darkness will always come to light.

We will always encounter evil people in this world, but trust your heart to overcome the obstacles.

If you concentrate your money in your business, your thoughts will centre on making the business profitable. If you direct the business to other people, you are concerned about their welfare.

Hypocrites describe people who do good acts for appearances only. Their actions may be good but their motives are hollow and don't plant good seeds for the next generation.

The word 'salt' should be remembered as making a difference in the world we live in, as salt changes the flavour and preserves food against decay.

From politicians to marketers, people use words to enhance positions or sell products and twist the meaning. It is not surprising that people "swear" to tell the truth.

When we depend on our Creator rather than our problems, he is able to offer help in unexpected ways.

"Love" – Our world is filled with words of love, including in popular songs, greeting cards, media counsellors and romantic novels, that shower us with dreams that can result in superficial feelings. Real Love is scarce; it is selfless giving, caring, sharing, and remembering the Creator who died for us. People focus on number one, which is generally themselves.

Hope in a fallen world.

When the wicked are in leadership in any organisation, whether a church, business, a family or government, the climate comes from the top.

Some people go to church, take communion, give money and let people know what they give to charities, but that is meaningless if we give for selfish reasons and not out of heartfelt LOVE.

Our children are gifts from the Creator and the Creator is concerned for their welfare as they put their trust in adults; make sure we do not cause distress or pain.

Sometimes, you encounter hostility in churches because people go there for the wrong reasons and the behaviour of the individual is not corrected. Hold on to your beliefs and you will attract the right people to strengthen you; this will become your family. Some people are entrenched in their own religious system and you will see these people for what they are as you are Holy Spirit-led not system-led.

Some people consult mediums and spiritualists to seek answers from dead people instead of knowing that the Creator is the only one that can give us eternal life, whose government is one of justice and peace and who is known as the Prince of Peace. Whenever we see the lights of Christmas, remember that this is our true light; don't focus on the Prince of Darkness.

Some people read the bible, pray in public and follow church rituals just to get noticed or honoured by showy spirituality. They like to walk around in flowing robes, flashy jewellery and be greeted and have the most important seats, but it's the people who do it out of LOVE, even behind closed doors, who are the honest ones.

A church building may be beautiful, but if the people are not sincere, the church will decay from within. How many empty churches do you know of? We should be deeply moved by the decay around us. A healthy loving church will always grow in numbers. One day, they will be led by the caring shepherd.

Going to church should not be like attending a memorial service and studying the bible like a historical document. He is alive and amongst the living through the Holy Spirit and if you try to live without him, you will be abandoning the purpose for which you were made.

The kind of prayers that get answered are those made by people who believe, not those who hold grudges, who ask out of selfish motives. Instead of thinking of the object of your request, seek peace and forgive others.

Good News:

Don't focus on trying to control your own destiny because what you have here on earth is only temporary; it cannot be exchanged for your soul. If you work hard at getting what you want, you might eventually have a pleasurable life, but in the end, you will find it hollow and empty.

We don't know the day or the hour when Jesus is coming back which is good news to those who trust in Him. 'Soon' means any moment and we must be ready, prepared for his return by making sure our efforts are used to better the world. This is terrible news for the ones who don't trust in the Creator of all things.

Parents' wrongdoings are often repeated by children unless the parent confesses the wrongdoing and carefully thinks and acts to put things right.

Parents want children to make the right decisions, but to do this, children must learn to make their own decisions. Making bad ones helps them make good ones. If parents make all the decisions, they leave their children without skills.

You can be forgiven for what you have done but you must be able to forgive others.

God created the universe so your life is not too complex for him to shine the light on your path to living a righteous life. He removes the darkness, and lives can be reborn spiritually to give you security in an insecure world. Think of it as a ladder to heaven.

Evil spirits or demons are ruled by Satan. They work to tempt people to cause wrongdoing. They were not created by Satan because God is the Creator.

Many people see church as entertainment. They enjoy the music, the people, and the activities but they forget why they are there which is to worship and for it to have an impact on their life. Some don't practice what they preach. There are true and false believers in churches.

What comes out of the mouth can damage people, so think before you speak. Ask yourself 'is what I am going to say true? Is it necessary? Is it kind?' Even if we may not achieve perfect control of our tongues, we can still learn enough control to reduce the damage our words can do.

Stop and think before you react or speak. If you control this small but powerful member, the tongue, you can control the rest of your body. The sharks of this world will always be swimming around you; however, be honest in your dealings and don't be their bait, and you will build resilience and gain strength.

Sometimes we have to be broken to rebuild a good character within us and be given a new heart.

Seeing with your eyes doesn't guarantee seeing with your heart.

Sometimes, hearts are permanently hardened because they don't want to change.

Don't be afraid:

When we suffer on earth, Satan cannot harm our souls or take away our right to eternal life as a believer. There are many reasons to be afraid here on earth because this is the devil's domain. But if you choose to follow the person who created you, he will give you everlasting safety.

The wicked may succeed for a while but evil will not remain unpunished; you reap what you sow.

Crooked judges and those who make unjust laws will eventually become powerless.

Evil people, who are just focused on their self-serving interests, will rot and decay.

Evil is a temporary condition in the Universe and will one day be destroyed.

People who genuinely follow the Creator, not because they think they are good: You are there for people who know they have failed and want help; these are the people with whom we need to build relationships that are longer lasting than those formed in our physical families.

We should never envy evil people, even if excessively rich or popular. No matter how much they have, it will fade and vanish like grass that withers and dies.

Although we cannot be sure why demonic possession occurs, we know that evil spirits can use the human body for distortion. Avoid all curiosity about or involvement with demonic forces or the occult. People are fascinated by horoscopes, fortune-telling, witchcraft and bizarre cults, but they cannot give you eternal life.

An evil action begins with a single thought. Our minds can dwell on lust and envy, hatred or revenge; instead, think about what is the right thing for our behaviour.

Doctors cure physical disease but the Creator cares more about what you fill your heart with and takes care of your soul.

It is not enough to be emptied of evil if we will not want the power of the Holy Spirit to give us a new purpose; washing your outsides will mean washing your insides.

Demons are powerful and destructive, although they are powerless over those who believe in eternal life. Therefore, if we resist the devil, he will leave us alone.

Don't be afraid; reach out in faith and that will heal your body, soul and spirit.

In our fallen world, disease and disability are common. Their causes are many, often multiple – inadequate nutrition, contact with a source of infection, lowered defences and even direct attack by Satan. Whatever the immediate cause of our illness, we can trace its original source to Satan, the author of all evil in this world.

Lions attack sick, young or struggling animals; they chose victims who are alone. Watch out for Satan when you are suffering and look to the Creator instead.

Reflection

Think of any problems in the past which have turned out for the good in the end.

Our society is addicted to pleasure and power, but these can quickly pass away. Look at your own talents and possessions and consider how to turn them into something good for the next generation. Don't be a captive and set yourself free.

Always remember, to change, we will sometimes fail. It will be hard work; we will be criticised but the reward will be so good in the end.

"What can I learn and how can I grow from my mistakes?" is better than "Who did this to me?"

Don't hate people, just hate what they do.

Even some churches and workplaces today have false people as leaders who have secretly slipped in to justify their own opinions, lifestyle, or wrong behaviour. They may gain temporary freedom, but all they are doing is playing with fire as they will be judged.

Realising life is short helps us use the time we have more wisely for eternal good.

The only words that you need:

God is sovereign. He is greater than any power in the universe. God is not compared with any leader, government, or religion. Throughout history, he has wanted for you to come to him through Christ. Christ came to earth as a "Lamb", the symbol of perfect sacrifice to sin, but He will return as the triumphant "Lion", the rightful ruler and conqueror. He will defeat Satan, settle accounts with all those who reject him and bring his faithful people to eternity. God will bring us a new heaven and earth. These promises will be fulfilled and can give us hope. Alpha and Omega – the beginning and the end.

If you are lying awake at night worrying about what you can't change, pour out your heart to the Creator and thank him that he is in control, and then sleep will come.

You are the books you read, the films you watch, the music you listen to, the people you spend time with, the conversation you engage in. Choose wisely what you feed your mind.

Reflect on what you spend the most of your time thinking about and how you invest the majority of your energy.

Now that you have learnt new behaviours and know that, if in a crisis, you have support, this must give you a sense of relief. We are not all experts in everything.

Reflection continued

True beauty begins inside.

We work hard to keep our outward appearance attractive, but what is in our heart is even more important. Seek healthy thoughts and motives, not just healthy food and exercise.

It is as hard to refuse to listen to gossip as it is to turn down a delicious dessert. Taking one morsel of either one creates a taste for more. If you don't nibble on the first bite then you can't take the second or third.

Satan is here now, however, and he is trying to win us over to his evil cause. With the power of the Holy Spirit, we can resist the devil and he will flee from us.

No matter what trials or persecutions you may face, your soul cannot be harmed.

You may not be able to keep people from slandering you, but you can at least stop supplying them with ammunition. As long as you do what is right, their accusations will be empty and only embarrass them.

We must be law-abiding citizens and pay our taxes to the government that is in power and what we owe to our debtors. Don't worry about corruption and greed; what we hear and experience of our government, that will be dealt with.

Don't gloat about someone's misfortune as that soon could be yours.

When you are hurting, depressed or broken, remember that there is someone you can reach out to who understands your humanity as he knows your background and failures. Just have faith; he is not a cosmic magician – he is the Master.

When people commit lustful affairs, they must remember that it is hurting others and destroying lives too.

A selfish person lives for themselves with little concern for how their actions affect others. This can contaminate the entire nation, so don't be part of this.

The rich person can lose all his material wealth, but no one can take away a poor person's character. Don't be jealous of the rich; money may be all they ever have.

We live in a materialistic society where many people serve money. They spend their time collecting and storing it only to die and leave it behind. The love of money is the root of all evil. One test is to ask yourself what occupies your thoughts more.

Some people think that it is youth, strength, power, wealth and pleasure that brings happiness today. They never focus on the unseen, which has the key to eternity.

Respect those who are older than us, listen to those who are younger than us and be humble enough that you can learn from each other.

We should do what we can to fight injustice of every sort.
___

Now you have had time to look back at your attitude and behaviour, how should your life change for the better?

Will the change affect your relationships and how will you now use your time and resources?

Our days are numbered and we should want our work to count. What one thing could I do this week to help a helpless person?

Think of what we doing now; is this helping or harming people and how are we going to use our resources? The issue is not what we have but how well we use what we have.

Whether we buy or sell, make a product, or offer a service, we know what is honest and what is dishonest. Sometimes we feel pressure to be dishonest in order to advance ourselves or gain more profit. Always seek honesty.

Write down your thoughts

_____
_____
_____
_____
_____
_____
_____
_____
_____
_____
_____
_____
_____
_____
_____
_____

What do I want to do in my life to make a difference before I die..............?

Don't pretend that you have learned from past history, when your present behaviour shows you have learned nothing. Practice what you preach.

It is good that we don't know when our world is going to be taken back. If we knew the correct date, we might be tempted to be lazy, so we need to get prepared now.

Preparation cannot be bought or borrowed at the last minute. We must be ready for our final journey as it will be swift and sudden.

Our time, abilities and money are not ours in the first place – we are caretakers, not owners. When we ignore and squander what we have on people who are not going to make a difference, what do you think we deserve?

Our next life is not physical or political; it is what is in our hearts.

His or her last words are very important; our finite minds cannot comprehend the infinite. It simply means that we will not be an extension of this life and that the same physical and natural rules won't apply.

What do you want to be remembered by? The words we leave behind will be a lasting picture of who we are.

Which is more important to you – what you get out of life, or what you put into it?

List what you want to do

_____
_____
_____
_____
_____

Words and actions

You have had words; are you going to put into action what you have written or reflected upon?

If you need songs to listen to when things are getting to you, you are not alone. You can use the words to think about what you have learnt about yourself and how this is going to make a difference. Think of your own songs where the words you have heard tugged at your heartstrings. Is this your destiny?

Artist	Title	Reference
CeeLo Green	Mary, Did You Know	(Film is worth watching; it's only the Creator you need)
Simon and Garfunkel	Bridge Over Troubled Water	(Building resilience by crying out if you need to)
Simon and Garfunkel	The Sound of Silence	(Personal relationship)
Sugababes	Caught in a Moment	(Go with your heart)
Billy Ocean	Suddenly	(Love comes from above)
Eva Cassidy	Songbird	(The Creator loves you)
Coldplay	Fix You	(Don't be afraid)
Jennifer Hudson	Spotlight	(When being controlled)
The O'Jays	Backstabbers	(Find trustful people and you will attract good people)

Eagles	Love Will Keep Us Alive	(You're not alone)
Gerry and the Pacemakers	You'll Never Walk Alone	(Give you hope)
Tom Baxter	Skybound	(Don't hide your love for the Creator; you can become one)
Roxy Music	Same Old Scene	(Anyone can turn the corner and be righteous)
Marmalade	Reflections of my Life	(Think of happy times)
Dream Theater	The Spirit Carries On	(Just believe; there is hope)
Elton John	Circle of Life	(We all have a place in this world and are unique to our fingertips)
Anthem Lights	How Great Thou Art	(Look at our creation; how beautiful it is. Take time and look at nature; the trees)

Songs continued

Luther Vandross	The Impossible Dream	(There is hope; justice will prevail)
Will Downing	A Love Supreme	(New beginning)
Gladys Knight & The Pips	Neither One of Us	(Ending relationships; sometimes we need to in order to function)
The Jacksons	Dreamer	(Focus on the unseen that can give you eternal life)
George Michael	This is Not Real Love	(Test the heart and real love will help you work through your relationship)
Jessie Ware	Save A Kiss	(Treat people with love and respect; kiss on the cheek when greeting)
Michael Jackson	Earth Song	(Respect the world we live in)
George McCrae	It's Been So Long	(Don't hold grudges)
Glenn Fry	You belong to the City	(Everyone deserves a new start)
Frankie goes to Hollywood	The Power of Love	(Everyone has a chance to be loved)
Sam Smith	Writing's on the Wall	(Don't run; focus on the unseen)
Moby	Why Does My Heart Feel So Bad	(Nobody can injure your heart and soul; still time to search)
Whitney Houston	All the Man That I Need	(Serve one master)

Gladys Knight and the Pips	You're the Best Thing That Ever Happened to Me	
George McCrae	It's Been So Long	(Forgiveness)
Muse	Uprising	(Corruption, dealt with)
Melanie C	I Turn to You	(Hope)
Rick Astley	Keep Singing	(You can be saved from throwing your life away)
George Michael	Jesus to a Child	(Unconditional love)
Stormzy	Blinded by your Grace	(Broken but can be fixed)

If you are visual, there are two true-life films that are all you ever need to watch to find peace in your life. They will capture your heart, capture your mind and ultimately impact your life forever as they are powerful and poignant.

Son Of God (Roma Downey)

Heaven is Real (From the New York Times #1 Bestseller)

Seek wisdom and righteousness

Unfortunately, people will use us to support their own motives and we will lose trust, but be kind to one another, be tender-hearted, forgiving each other, just as the Creator shows also in Christ who forgave you.

Remember the tree as a symbol and what it is made out of. Christ was born in a manger, was a carpenter and died on the Cross, but trees don't need humans to live to experience everlasting life. Just believe and let everything you do be done in LOVE.

For more information on no-jargon questions about the Creator of the universe, just read the Life Application Bible, as this wonderful Creator wants a relationship with you.

The Creator knocks on everyone's door but sometimes the door doesn't open because the fear of feeling not worthy or a lack of understanding can become a problem.

Everyone has a flicker within but it is up to the person if they want to ignite it or not. The bible is not a collection of human ideas about God; it is God's very words given through people to people.

You do not have to go to church to learn about the Creator either. He can be with you through the Holy Spirit. However, be around good people who honestly share the beliefs, as these people will only worship one master, not materialism, self-importance, or any idols that have false symbolism.

www.ingramcontent.com/pod-product-compliance
Lightning Source LLC
Chambersburg PA
CBHW020914080526
44589CB00011B/599